The New Earth Series Presents

Sustainable Solutions for a Successful Business

By

Dr. Enid Alane Thompson

Published by CreateSpace Self-Publishing (LLC), an Amazon Company, and Kindle

Direct Publishing (LLC) Copyright of Book is held by the Author.

2016

All Rights Reserved

Dedication

All my work is dedicated to my family, friends, and for anyone who desires to make a positive change in the world.

Sustainable Solutions for a Successful Business- A look at the Starbucks Corporation

Dr. Enid A. Thompson analyzed the Starbucks Corporation's sustainability in the coffee industry. This Sustainable Solutions Report (SSR) contains two competitive companies in the coffee industry. In addition, contains (a) stakeholder identification and value analysis, (b) enterprise level strategy, (c) organizational culture, (d) integrated concepts from reading, evidence, and implications, (e) general forces analysis, (f) economics, (g) technology, (i) demographics/ social/culture. The concentration of this SSR addresses the gap between the Starbucks Corporation's ability to design and implement sustainable value creation strategies for increasing profitability and maximizing shareholder value.

The Starbucks Corporation is a major firm operating in the coffee industry. Founded in 1971 the headquarters is located in Seattle, Washington. The Starbucks Corporation is a *"Fortune 500 Company"*. In 2012, the firm ranked number 21and currently ranked 19 on Forbes Global 2000 Leading Companies as innovative. Moreover, Starbucks was ranked 76 as world's most valuable Brands (Forbes, 2013). The Starbuck's Corporation lead by Howard Schultz is on the move. Mr. Schultz successfully translated the vision of building a *"performance-driven company through the lens of humanity"* into measurable goals and objectives that have been met through innovation and ethical behavior (Starbucks, 2014).

Executive Summary

The Starbucks Corporation is the world leader in the retail coffee industry. This Sustainable Solutions Report (SSR) summarizes the firms' position in the coffee industry. As the world leader in the coffee business, Starbucks sustains its competitive advantage over its' rivals. Reaching over 40,000 stores worldwide the multinational organization focuses on three main elements. The three elements are providing a matchless list of goods, supreme customer service, and providing continuous improvement in quality.

The Starbucks mission is *"to inspire and nurture the human spirit – one person, one cup and one neighborhood at a time."* (Starbucks, 2014). In fiscal 2013, Starbucks consolidated revenues reached a record $14.9 billion, a 12 percent increase over last year was driven by a 7 percent rise in global comparable store sales and the opening of 1,701 net new stores around the globe. Starbucks non-GAAP operating income was $2.5 billion, a 23 percent increase, with record non-GAAP operating margin of 16.5 percent, an impressive 150 basis points higher than last year. This strong revenue growth, coupled with excellent margin improvement, led to record non-GAAP earnings per share of $2.26, up 26 percent over fiscal 2012. Through dividends and share repurchases, Starbucks returned a record $1.2 billion of cash to shareholders (Starbucks, 2014).

Today, Starbucks brand is strong, diverse, and well known all over the world. In addition, there are more than 200,000 collaborates supporting the firms' success of their bold strategic vision; dedication to disruptive innovation, operational excellence; and a foundation of strong values. The leadership of Starbucks understands the importance of communicating their vision, maintaining focus on stakeholders, and providing quality products and service. The firms' recent technology rollout of the "Mobile App" is creating a wave of interest with consumers and other rival firms.

Summary of Key Takeaways and Insights

      The Starbucks Corporation key takeaways from the results of each analysis reflect the firm's current strategy aligns with the theories and frameworks outlined in this SSB. The level of success ranges from low to high. Starbucks has a high level of success aligning strategy. However, there are medium levels of success for the General Forces Analysis and Key Success Factors: Integrating the Analysis (see Table 1). Focusing on improving both areas will increase short-term cost-effectiveness and future sustainability.

Name of Analysis or Assessment	Starbucks results indicate current strategy aligns with theory (YES or NO)? How successful is alignment (Low, Medium, or High level)
Stakeholder Identification and Value Analysis	YES. High level of success.
General Force Analysis	YES. Medium level of success.
Porter's Five Forces Industry Analysis	YES. Medium level of success.
Detailed Value Chain Analysis	YES. High level of success.
Key Success Factors: Integrating the Analysis	YES. Medium level of success.
Analyzing the Company Strategy Type	YES. High level of success.
Analyzing the Company Strategy Moves	YES. High level of success.
Alignment & Goals Analysis	YES. High level of success.
Fitness Landscape Translation Analysis	YES. High level of success.
Boid Analysis	YES. High level of success.
Industry Evolution Modeling	YES. High level of success.
Life- Cycle Assessment (LCA)	YES. High level of success.
Compliance to Innovation Analysis	YES. High level of success.
Sustainable Value Framework Synthesis: Detailed Driver Analysis	YES. High level of success

Stakeholder Identification and Value Analysis

Stakeholder analysis is systematically identifying key stakeholders and judgment that influences the high growth and strategies that support sustainability (Laureate, 2012). Stakeholders of a firm like Starbucks are enormous and knowing their stakeholders in each area is vital. The areas requiring a focus on the stakeholders of Starbucks are the internet, human capital, and knowledge management, roles of teams and virtual teams, value-driven growth models, a new paradigm for boards of directors, profit zone analysis, and globalization (Starbucks, 2014).

Traditionally, stakeholders were considered as the owners of the firm, board members, key customers, suppliers, and top management. In today's business environment-defining stakeholders includes large blocks of profitable customers or persons in need of the services or products that a firm offers. Also, this could lead to breakthrough growth (Press, 2005). The leadership of Starbucks does a good job of listening to their stakeholders.

The Starbucks brand creates value. Starbucks, known all over the world and can sell products that their competitors are not able to market. For example, the firm sells a variety of coffee brands. In addition, the firm sells coffee-related materials such as coffee mugs, thermoses, grinders, and glasses being their name logo. The competitors are not able to match Starbucks. The rivals have not established themselves internationally as Starbucks has. Marketing and Product Differentiation are strategic strengths of Starbucks and sets them apart from the competition (Press, 2005).

Other linkages of value considered when analyzing Starbucks include a choice of store locations and partnerships. Starbucks stores are located close to shopping centers, which increases exposure and access. Starbucks layout itself is strategic in nature. Also, Starbucks collaborates with many airports, stores such as Barnes & Noble's exclusively, and hotel conglomerates like Marriott and Hilton. Dunkin Donuts and other competitors do not have an answer for how Starbucks commands the industry. Starbucks has transformed the way people consume coffee beverages converting it into a pleasurable experience (Marriott, 2007).

Another opportunity for Starbucks is teaming with hotels to offer the firm's coffee packages in the rooms. Offering coffee packages may not necessarily turn into a source of great income for the coffee giant. However, it does expand their exposure to many others who do not drink their beverages thus, increasing the exposure for the firm's brand (Marriott, 2007).

Enterprise Level Strategy

The Starbucks Corporation is a progressive firm on the move. The mission of the firm is *"to inspire and nurture the human spirit – one person, one cup and one neighborhood at a time"* (Starbucks, 2014). The leadership of Starbucks values their employees and the service they provide. Enterprise Level Strategy is a form of strategy within a firm and deals with issues that affect the organization; usually developed at the highest level within the firm (Laureate, 2012). As mentioned early a stakeholder is the internet, human capital, and knowledge management, roles of teams and virtual teams, value-driven growth models, a new paradigm for boards of directors, profit zone analysis, and globalization (Starbucks, 2014).

Organizational Culture Type

Organizational structure and organizational culture are interconnected. The definition of organizational culture is a system of assumptions, values, norms, and attitudes manifested through symbols that members of the firm developed through mutual experience (Janićijević, 2013). Organizational structure is relatively stable, either planned or spontaneous; the patterns of actions and interactions that organization's members undertake for achieving the organizational goals.

The Starbucks Corporation leadership exhibits an understanding of both definitions well. The firm is about value, respect, diversity, and inclusion (Starbucks, 2014). The leadership behaves in a manner that demonstrates strong ethical behavior and inclusion. Also, the leadership works and thinks across teams, functions, and businesses. The firm considers other markets, channels, and communities across the physical and digital spaces (Starbucks, 2014).

Starbucks is unique due to these groups providing insight on product innovation, business solutions, and collaborate on partner development. The leadership team emphases diversity and inclusion that (a) build a diverse workforce, (b) increase cultural competencies, (c) shape a culture of inclusion, and (d) develop a diverse network of suppliers (Forbes, 2013).

Integrated Concepts from Readings, Evidence, and Implications

The implications of the research provide a picture of a culture type for the Starbucks Corporation. The firm is unique and a major leader in the coffee industry. Starbucks competitive advantage and the relationship between leadership and the subordinate staff are strong. The vital parts of research are the descriptions, analyses, and interpretations of the data. The implication of the research is equally important. The research findings identify for the reader why and how the culture supports diversity and inclusion of the firm. Moreover, the way key concepts in the analysis have evolved. Also, the evidence supports assertions or the interpretations presented (Stainback, 1988).

General Force Analysis: External – Remote Environment

This section of the SSR examines the threats and opportunities affecting the Starbucks Corporation external environment. The general external forces include analyzing the five forces in the external environment. The five categories of forces in the external environment are (a) economics, (b) demographics, (c) government/legal/military, (d) physical environment, (e) technology (Pearce, 2003).

The Starbucks Corporation conducts business in the coffee and snack industry. The coffee industry sector is in the mature stage of its lifecycle with a medium level concentration. Starbucks holds 36.7% in market share (IBIS World: The Coffee & Snack Shop Industry, 2014). Since 1999, the coffee and snack industry has grown due to consumer spending and an increase in disposable incomes. However, in 2009 Starbucks experienced a decrease in revenue due to the economic crisis in the United States.

General Force Matrix Analysis

Economics. The current stock market value is $51.64 Billion and highest stock value as of July 12, 2014, was $74.23 (Brain, 2014). With approximately 151,000 employees, the firm earned 13.29 Billion in 2012. There is a large demand for coffee beans. Weather is a contributing factor in the coffee bean industry and can affect pricing.

Technology. The firm introduced the computerized coffee roasters that offer consistency in the taste of their coffee. The new technology increase customer retention and customer satisfaction (Starbucks, 2014). The advance agricultural technology produces high quality of the coffee bean.

Demographics / social / culture. Starbucks is the largest coffeehouse company in the world, with 23,187 stores in 64 countries, including 12,973 in the United States, 1,897 in China, 1,550 in Canada, 1,088 in Japan and 927 in the United Kingdom. Social- Coffee becomes a popular beverage around the world. Also, coffee satisfied the attitude of leisure life. Portable coffee fits a fast pace lifestyle (Starbucks, 2014).

Government / legal / military. Due to the Affordable Healthcare Law, insurance coverage for the Starbucks Corporation has increased. The firm was one of the first U.S. retailers to offer health coverage to eligible full-time and part-time employees and their families. Starbucks has developed tools and resources to explain the firm's responsibilities to their partners (Starbucks, 2014). Adhering to labor and employment regulations the firm displayed a high level of corporate responsibility by providing their employees' healthcare insurance immediately.

Physical environment. Unpredictable events such as the economic crisis of 2008 affected Starbucks revenue. The firm closed over 300 stores due to profits dropping 69 percent in the first quarter of 2009 (Miller, 2009). However, the move to close the 300 stores give the company the ability to reform and create other opportunities to gain more market share.

Implications, Threats, and Opportunities of GFA

The implications of the research provided a picture of the coffee industry, the major competitors in the industry, Starbucks competitive advantage, and the relationship between coffee consumption and health. The vital parts of research were the descriptions, analyses, and interpretations of the data. The implication of the research was equally important. The research findings contained descriptions of the why and how the analyses and interpretations came together. Moreover, the way key concepts in the analyses have evolved. As the researcher, I outlined the patterns that emerged from the data and reported a range of evidence that supported the claims and interpretations presented (Stainback, 1988).

Porter's Five Forces Industry Analysis: External – Industry Environment

Porter's Five Forces framework analyzes and supports strategy development. The five areas are Threat of New Entrants, Threat of Substitutes, Bargaining Power of Buyers, Bargaining Power of Suppliers, and Intensity of Competitive Rivalry (Press, 2005). Porter's Five Forces are useful for understanding an analytical grasp of the completion and the essential economics in industry. The Threat of New Entrants for Starbucks was low. The market is saturated, and large amounts of financial resources associated with building and properties were required to enter the industry.

The Threat of Substitutes was high. Many beverage choices are available for substituting coffee. Which include tea, fruit juices, water, soda, and energy drinks. Pubs and Bars also serve as alternatives meeting places outside of home or work environments. Bargaining Power of Buyers was high. Starbucks offered little or no cost switching for customers. Bargaining Power of Suppliers was high. The demand for coffee beans is high due to coffee beans can only be produced in certain geographical areas. The Intensity of Competitive Rivalry is high. Starbucks has competitors like McDonald's, Dunkin Donuts, Costa, and Caribou that provide local coffee shops and cafes.

Five Forces Matrix Analysis

Barriers to Entry - Low		
Substitutes	High	
Bargaining power of suppliers - High	**Bargaining power of buyers -** High	**Competitive Rivalry** High

Dunkin' Donuts and McDonald's are Starbucks' competitors each are quick-serve restaurant selling premium coffee. Recently, both rivals announced that the weather was the major contributor to weakened sales (Yaqalla, 2014). Dunkin Donuts opened its door for business in 1950 by the owner Bill Rosenberg. The store was located in Quincy Massachusetts. The firm obtained licensing for franchising in 1955. (Dunkin' Donuts, 2011). The McDonald's Corporation was founded by Ray Kroc, Dick, and Mac McDonald in 1955 (McDonald's Corporation, 2014). Below is the financial standing for each firm.

	Market Cap	Forward P/E	Price/Sales	1 Year Return	Dividend Yield
Starbucks	$54.01B	22.54	3.50	17.94%	1.5%
McDonald's	$99.71B	16.09	3.52	(1.42%)	3.2%
Dunkin' Brands	$4.95B	22.15	6.96	20.68%	1.9%

Implications, Threats, and Opportunities of Porter's Five Forces

Experts (i.e., economist) stated that the next five years Starbucks and its competitor Dunkin Donuts will increase their international operations to capitalize on emerging markets abroad (IBIS World: The Coffee & Snack Shop Industry, 2014). Over the next five years to 2019, industry value added (IVA), which measures an industry's contribution to GDP, is projected to grow at an annual rate of 4.3% per year. During the same period, GDP estimates growth at an annualized rate of 2.7%, meaning the industry is growing at a slightly faster rate than the overall economy (IBIS World: The Coffee & Snack Shop Industry, 2014).

The Starbucks Corporation has big plans for the future. The leadership team at the firm recently changed. The goals of the coffee retailer are going beyond its original model of bricks and mortar to digital and mobile technology (Johnson, 2014). The strategy of the Starbucks Corporation is to increase its market share. Critics stated that during a conference call on Wednesday, January 31, 2014, Howard Schultz, CEO of Starbucks revealed a new leadership structure that puts mobile and digital at the center of how the retailer plans to build its business going forward (Johnson, 2014).

Starbucks can expand its' presence in the emerging markets. With the saturation of the US market having an international strategy is vital. Expanding the product mix and offerings with the introduction of the firm's tea and fresh juice offerings was a smart move. Starbucks has the opportunity for future monetizes its brand. Technology advances is a growing field, and the firm is currently leveraging the use of mobile applications.

New distribution channels - Starbucks recently introduced their new technology called

"Mobile Pour" in a beta test (Starbucks, 2014). Changing consumer taste and lifestyle is a challenge. Consumers are moving toward healthy products, and the current coffee culture could become a fad. Developed countries economy can limit opportunities for Starbucks. In 2008, the recession caused the decreased in revenue; price volatility in the global coffee arena that Starbucks is unable to control. Increased competition is a large concern for Starbucks. Because the firm is in the mature stage of the lifecycle competitors like Dunkin Donut and McDonald's are gaining market share with their low prices and other offerings (IBIS World: The Coffee & Snack Shop Industry, 2014)

Detailed Value Chain Analysis: Internal Environment

Technology has a significant role in changing how firms conduct business with other companies, suppliers, consumers, and competitors. Technology affects industry structures support cost, and differentiation strategies (Porter, 1985). The value chain and technology add value to production, marketing, and the provision of after-sales service. What is vital to remember is that information technology in a competitive environment is the *"value chain."* Knowing understanding how a firm separates activities into the economically and technologically ways of doing business is critical. The separation of the two activities is called *"Value Activities"* (Porter, 1985).

The value chain is transforming. The newly industrialized countries such as Brazil and China are finding out that the traditional competitive paradigms are no longer sufficient (Albors-Garrigos, 2014). The value chain dynamics have three dimensions in the value chain. The three dimensions are flow or structure of inputs and outputs, geographic extension, and governance (Albors-Garrigos, 2014).

Governance is important because it determines the control various individuals or groups in the value chain exert activities taking place. The types of governance in the value chain are market, balanced network, directed network, and hierarchy. This cast of agents and actors must support the main and subordinate activities regarding innovation, financial support, knowledge dissemination, networking, education, and training (Albors-Garrigos, 2014).

The leadership team at the Starbucks Corporation understands that the employees are valuable. The leadership is committed to investing in their employees. Starbucks leadership believes that when employees are satisfied, they provide quality service. Starbucks infrastructure has various support systems such as human resources management, technology, and procurement (Starbucks, 2014). The primary activities of the firm are *inbound logistics*, which consist of sourcing coffee from diverse coffee beans producers. *Operations* as they have operations in 60 countries. Starbuck has a reputation for its progressive labor practices. Zack Huston representative for Starbucks said, *"it wanted to improve the "stability and consistency" in weekly work hours and amend some problems with the scheduling software"* (Starbucks, 2014). The expectation set by management regarding day-to-day operations focuses on excellence. The firm's comprehensive efforts to ensure an ethical workplace outline Starbucks Standards of Business Conduct located on the firm's website.

Outbound logistics are- (a) where the products mix sales in-store and some through large box retailers. Payment around source through the point of sale prepaid Starbucks Cards and mobile payments. *Marketing and Sales –* (b) are driven by the 'Starbucks Experience.' The reputation of excellent customer service with high-quality products is main factors. *Service* – (c) Starbucks reputation for providing the best service to consumers resonates around the world.

Starbucks is successfully executing their social media marketing plan. Starbucks marketing strategy is making social media a difference maker (Starbucks, 2014). The strategy Starbucks utilizes has a significant role in the firm's growth. The firm remained with the upper-scale of the coffee market, competing on comfort rather than convenience. Starbucks did a superior job quickly inserting itself into the American urban landscape (Times, 2014).

The firm focuses on original product bundling that includes great coffee, quality service, and a nice environment. Starbucks is in the lead position in social media using Twitter, Facebook, Pinterest, G+, YouTube, and My Starbucks Ideas (Starbucks, 2014). The firm has embraced the digital age. The Howard Schultz contributes the success of *"the firm to Starbucks team ability to wear so many hats"* (Forbes, 2013). The firm's sales increased 11% in July of 2014, with a share surge of 22% to a Q3 record of $0.67 (Starbucks, 2014).

Firm Infrastructure- Starbucks have well designed, aesthetically pleasing stores. They have an efficient level of finance; accounting and legal departments to support the firm's infrastructure- *Human Resource Management* – Great benefits, employee empowerment, and amazing corporate culture makes Starbucks drive efficient management of human capital. Managing human capital effectively leaders must realize employees need to feel valued. Howard Schultz the CEO believes that *"the employees of the Starbuck Corporation should feel appreciated"* (Starbucks, 2014). Compensation plans like performance bonuses and employee stock ownership help in retention of employees. Moreover, emphasizing an open-door policy with management is part of the culture. A wide range of training and development programs are available for the staffs which can motivate them, including tangible and intangible incentives. Specifically, in the UK Starbucks staffs are entitled to free drinks during the shift (Starbucks, 2014). *Technology development* – Investments in innovative technologies like the well like a mobile app. Cost savings is one of the core objectives at Starbucks. The firm depends on technology to support this objective. Also, to relying on technology for cost savings the firm uses technology for ensuring their products quality and customer experience is superior (Starbucks, 2014). The firm introduced the computerized coffee roasters that offer consistency in the taste of their coffee. The new technology increase customer retention and customer satisfaction (Starbucks, 2014). The firm is one of the industries leaders in innovation (Forbes, 2013). *Procurement* - Starbucks obtains their products from a diverse group of a supplier with fixed contracts. Procurement is the purchasing of items needed for the production of products and services offered by a firm. For the Starbucks Corporation, coffee beans, and raw food items fit the description. Another area related to procurement is buildings and machinery (Starbucks, 2014).

The demand for Starbucks coffee and other products the firm offers is determined by factors including attitudes regarding health, the price of coffee on the world market, disposable income, and demographics (IBIS, 2014). Using Porter's Five Forces Analysis Starbucks Threat of New Entrants is moderate, Threat of Substitutes is high, Bargaining Power of Buyers moderate to low pressure, Bargaining Power of Suppliers low to moderate pressure, and last the Intensity of Competitive Rivalry is high to moderate (Starbucks, 2014).

Customized Value Chain of Activities in Table Form Table 1: Value Chain Analysis

Business Process	Your Organization	McDonalds
Management	The Starbucks Corporation teams of leaders are diverse and innovative. Together they embrace diversity to create a place where employees can be themselves. Respect and dignity are cornerstones of the firm.	McDonald's leadership is currently experiencing problems with employee's retention and unfair wage practices (Washington Post, 2014).
R&D	Starbucks expenses for research and development costs are extraordinary. The company spent approximately $20.7 million during fiscal years 2008, 2007, and 2006, on technical research and development activities. Also, the routine product testing, product, and process improvements in all areas of its business are paramount. (Starbucks, 2014)	
HR	Great benefits, employee empowerment, and amazing corporate culture enables Starbucks to drive efficient management of human capital. Managing human capital effectively, leaders must realize employees need to feel valued. Howard Schultz the CEO believes that *"the employees of the Starbuck Corporation should feel appreciated"* (Starbucks, 2014). Compensation plans like performance bonuses and employee stock ownership help in the retention of their employees. Moreover, emphasizing an open-door policy with management is part	

	of the culture. A wide range of training and development programs are available for the staffs which can motivate them, including tangible and intangible incentives. Specifically, in the UK Starbucks staffs are entitled to free drinks during the shift (Starbucks, 2014). *Technology development* – Investments in innovative technologies like the well like a mobile app. Cost savings is one of the core objectives at Starbucks. The firm depends on technology to support this objective. Also, to relying on technology for cost savings the firm uses technology for ensuring their products quality and customer experience is superior (Starbucks, 2014). The firm introduced the computerized coffee roasters that offer consistency in the taste of their coffee. The new technology increase customer retention and customer satisfaction (Starbucks, 2014). The firm is one of the industries leaders in innovation (Forbes, 2013).	
Procurement	Starbucks obtains products from a diverse group of the supplier. Also, has fixed contracts with some of the suppliers. Procurement is the purchasing of items needed for the production of products and services offered by a firm. For the Starbucks Corporation, coffee beans, and raw food items fit the description.	Not Available

	Another area related to procurement is buildings and machinery (Starbucks, 2014)	
Inbound logistics	Strength	Weakness
Operations	Strength	Weakness
Outbound logistics	Where the product mix sales in-store and some through large box retailers. Payment around source through the point of sale prepaid Starbucks Cards and mobile payments.	Weakness
Sales	Driven by the 'Starbucks Experience."	Equal
Service	Strength	Weakness

Implications of Competitive Analysis

Strengths- Starbucks is the leader among competitors like Dunkin Donuts and McDonalds. The brand of Starbucks is renowned. The Starbucks Corporation has big plans for the future. The leadership team at the firm recently changed. The goals of the coffee retailer are going beyond its original model of bricks and mortar to digital and mobile technology (Johnson, 2014). The strategy of the Starbucks Corporation is to increase its market share. Critics stated that during a conference call on Wednesday, January 31, 2014, Howard Schultz, CEO of Starbucks revealed a new leadership structure that puts mobile and digital at the center of how the retailer plans to build its business going forward (Johnson, 2014).

Weaknesses- The unpredictability of coffee prices and the economy could pose a threat. Experts state that the next five years Starbucks and its competitor Dunkin Donuts will increase their international operations to capitalize on emerging markets abroad (IBIS World: The Coffee & Snack Shop Industry, 2014). Over the next five years to

2019, industry value added (IVA), which measures an industry's contribution to GDP, is projected to grow at an annual rate of 4.3% per year. During the same period, GDP estimates growth at an annualized rate of 2.7%, meaning the industry is growing at a slightly faster rate than the overall economy (IBIS World: The Coffee & Snack Shop Industry, 2014).

Detailed SWOT Analysis

Assets and return measure a firm's strengths and weaknesses. Every business must have a method for evaluating their internal weaknesses and strengths (Press, 2005). Getting to the core of many different perceptions, the firm needs a method that incorporates a variety of observations. Organizing collective intelligence is vital. Expanding the SWOT analysis to include individuals or groups outside the firm to gain a true picture is important. Once the steps are completed, the SWOT team must compile the findings in a formal report. The report will benefit senior management, strategic planners, and other interested parties (Press, 2005). Evaluating the strengths and weakness of the firm's core competencies provides the foundation for new or revised strategies.

Strengths: Strong Market Position and Global Brand Recognition: Starbucks has a significant geographical presence across the globe, maintain a 36.7% market share in the United States, and has operations in over 60 countries. Starbucks is also the most recognized brand in the coffeehouse segment and is ranked 91st in the best global brands of 2013 (Starbucks, 2014). Starbucks effectively leverages its rich brand equity by merchandising products, licensing its brand logo out. Such strong market position and brand recognition allow the company to gain significant competitive advantage in further expanding into international markets and help register higher growth in both domestic and international markets (Times, 2014). Over the years, they have achieved significant economies of scale with superior distribution channels and supplier relationships. Products of the Highest Quality: They give the highest importance to the quality of their products and avoid standardization of their quality even for higher production output.

Weaknesses: Expensive Products: While Starbucks does differentiate their products with being highly quality couple with the whole 'Starbucks Experience,' in times of economic sluggishness, consumers to have such switching costs to competitor's products with lower prices and forgo paying a premium (Starbucks, 2014). These premium prices could also pose some weakness for it to succeed in developing countries.

Opportunities: Expansion into Emerging Markets: The increase saturation of the US market makes its international strategy even more important. Starbucks has made a good inroad into many countries, with India recently joining the list with a joint venture entry. Starbucks has a great growth potential in further expanding into the emerging and developing markets. They can leverage their size, experience, financial prowess, and efficiencies to make new market share.

Threats: Increased Competition: This is by far the biggest threat that Starbucks faces with the market being at a mature stage, there is increased pressure on Starbucks from its competitors like Dunkin Brands, McDonald's, Costa Coffee, Pete's Coffee, mom and pop specialty coffee stores. Dunkin Brands had at its main threat in the US market by trailing Starbucks with a 24.6% share. Price Volatility in the Global Coffee Market: There have been significant fluctuations in the market prices of high-quality coffee beans, which Starbucks cannot control. Developed Countries Market Saturation: Starbucks derives a significant amount of its revenue from the development markets, and there is increased market saturation currently. Developed Countries Economy: In an increasingly economically integrated world, an economic crisis like the one in 2008 could have a trickle-down effect from the developed markets to the developing markets. This threat would hurt revenues for Starbucks as consumers shift away from premium product mix to stay in limited budgets during economic hardships. Changing the consumer's tastes and lifestyle choices entail (a) the shift of consumers toward more healthy products, and (b) the risk of coffee culture being just a fad represent a threat for Starbucks going into the future (Starbucks, 2014).

SO strategies - Starbucks can expand its present in the emerging markets. With the saturation of the US market having an international strategy is vital. Starbucks has opportunities for future monetizes its brand. Technology advances is a growing field, and the firm is currently leveraging the use of mobile applications. New distribution channels- Starbucks recently introduced their new technology called "Mobile Pour" in a beta test (Starbucks, 2014).

ST Strategies - Changing consumer taste and lifestyle is a challenge. Consumers are moving toward healthy products, and the current coffee culture could become a fad. Developed countries economy can limit opportunities for Starbucks. In 2008, the recession caused the decreased in revenue. Increased competition is a large concern for Starbucks because the firm is in the mature stage of the lifecycle. Competitors like Dunkin Donut and McDonald's are gaining market share with their low prices and other offerings (IBIS World: The Coffee & Snack Shop Industry, 2014).

Key Success Factor Analysis

In order, for success to occur in business a firm must have a plan. Strategic planning and strategic intent thinking are vital. The topic strategic planning has been around for years, since the 1960's. Strategic planning includes every part of the firm, the employees, culture, and organizational arrangements (Mintzberg, 1999). Strategic planning should be a living organism; it must evolve as the firm grows.

Successful firms move forward by creative leaders and subordinates who are open and understand the end goal. Calling strategic planning traditional in my opinion is like saying babies do not grow up. There is nothing anything traditional about strategic planning for an organization. Each firm works differently and possesses different kinds of talented employees. The objective might be the same (i.e., to dominate the market) however, the approach to secure that lofty goal comes in many different forms.

The definition of "traditional" is orthodox, usual, routine, fixed or set, and habitual (Merriam-Webster, 2014). As I stated early, there is nothing traditional regarding strategic planning. For firms to succeed, strategic planning must change with the current environment of the firm. A firm must understand its' environment before engaging in the development of a competitive strategy, and this entails strategic intent thinking.

Strategic thinking drives new ideas on purpose. The strategy continues as a controversial topic and practice (Markides, 2012). Every firm needs a strategic plan; the surprising discovery is some firms are clueless about where to begin (Markides, 2012). Going beyond the rhetoric two main schools of thought on what strategy is are Michael

Porter's work and another main school of thought considers positioning to be 'static' and old news (Markides, 2012).

Strategic intent thinking involves planning. Effective strategies are developed by brainstorming, collaboration, and through trial and error. The strategy has to be thought-out and planned at a general level. On the other hand, it must remain flexible and adaptable to new learning and changes in the market environment (Markides, 2012). Strategic intent thinking is a combination of rational thinking, creativity, and analysis.

The strategic planning process and the strategic intent thinking must be measurable. The leadership of a firm will know how well their strategy works by the results produced by the implementation of each. Any outcome that falls below a predetermined goal should provoke leaders to look at external environments for threats and opportunities (Press, 2005). As stated earlier strategic planning should be a living organism, it must evolve as the firm grows. Strategic intent thinking should always be in front of the leadership's mind.

Analyzing the Company Strategy Type

A winning strategy must fit the firm's external and internal situations, build sustainable competitive advantage, and improve the firm's performance (Laureate, 2012). The Starbucks corporation strategy type does just that. The firm's strategy type is "Product Differentiation." Product differentiation makes Starbucks unique and sets the firm apart from its competitors. Product differentiation can outcompete rivals based on such differentiating features as higher quality, wider product selection, added performance, better service, attractive styling, technological superiority, and unusually good value for the cost (Press, 2005).

The value added by the firm through selling their products to consumers allows them to charge a premium cost for beverages and food products. The highest quality materials and standards produce Starbucks varied product selection (Starbucks, 2014). The firm selected the correct strategy type and will continue to provide superior products and services to consumers.

Action Plan Analysis

Over the next year, the Starbucks Corporation would benefit from fair trade green coffee importing cooperatives. The focus is on outreach programs and the environment. Consumers think this is important. This proposal supports research to find out if this or any other coffee cooperatives are threats to Starbucks. The next five years the cost of coffee will be a factor. Coffee cooperatives that provide gourmet coffee at a better price that is organic, and benefiting the environment, they are a threat to Starbucks. Since the economic crisis of 2008, consumers are not spending as they did (Brain, 2014). The spending trends on gourmet coffee must factor in the price for Starbucks over time.

Starbucks sustainable supply chain must continue to meet its demands by utilizing best business practices and focusing on tracking the demand in real time for next 12 months. The firm's green company takes pride in adhering to their policies and procedures to provide real-time production updates to their distributors, transportation information, and ethical issues. Providing coffee to communities all over the world, Starbucks major goal is to inspire and nurture (Starbucks, 2014).

The firm must concentrate on increasing their tenure in the industry. Focusing on corporate governance, business ethics, and compliance to ensure solid tenure over the five years is vital. Also, expanding into the Chinese market by creating a higher demand for the firm's products and services is currently in the works. One of the best practices used deals with Starbucks is the ability to reframe from downgrading the tea industry that has seniority in China. Their brand integrity has provided the opportunity to recruit and retain employees that uphold the firm's global brand (NetMBA, 2010).

Boid Analysis

The Boid Analysis identifies the three procedures leading the retail industry and the Starbucks Corporation. Customer focus and adding to the product mix that adds value is the first. Second, is matching price and promotions by having flexible pricing and promotion structure. The third is a move towards adopting global cultural changes while shaping and adopting consumer preference changes. Also, to changes to specific culture or countries that have operating units.

The analysis refers to *Boid as* homogeneous agents, which are autonomous entities interacting with other agents to produce an emerging whole system of patterns, for organizations as the industry (Stacey, 2011). To maintain order in the industry, all agents engage in unplanned interactions with a small number of other agents while following the same three basic, fundamental behavioral rules (Stacey, 2011).

Industry Evolution Modeling

The Starbucks Corporation is the leader in the retail coffee industry. The firm continues to evolve and match while shaping the coffee industry. Recently, Starbucks introduce the firm's new mobile application to customers in New York and San

Francisco. The new mobile app allows customers to order and prepay for their coffee and other products (Starbucks, 2014). The firm is on the move and quickly leaving the rivals behind.

Life Cycle Assessment

The leadership at Starbucks understands the larger picture. The management teams work to minimize downstream and upstream risks and environmental impacts caused by its operations (Starbucks, 2014). Through the lens of Life Cycle Assessment (LCA), a technique designed to assess environmental impacts of all the stages of a product's life from-cradle-to-grave, the question reveals a complex set of tradeoffs that the process examines a clear and unbiased fashion.

An example would be the benefit of the reusable cup. The benefit depends on some life cycle factors. Factor such as the average number of uses it gets as well as the impacts of the plastic used in its production. Moreover, what about the boiling water that Starbucks has pledged? The firm pledged to use boiled water to clean the cup before reuse (Starbucks, 2014). The firm will need to get that cup extremely clean to avoid cross-contamination of germs and negative human health impacts.

A *Life Cycle Assessment* (LCA) is a strategic management tool to see the larger representation of complexity surrounding organizations. LCA examines the downstream risks and upstream environmental impacts of a product, service, or organizational process from beginning to ending stages, and beyond (Senge, et al., 2010). According to Senge, Smith, Kruschwitz, Laur, & Schley (2010) LCA includes comparing like technologies and tracking technological breakthroughs, to continue redesigning products, services, or organizational processes (Senge, et al., 2010). LCA seeks to cultivate a synopsis of materials, while simultaneously creating a perspective inclusive of multiple life cycle stages and the manifold of environmental concerns (Senge, et al., 2010).

Society continues to make a demand for reductions in carbon footprints, and LCA modeling can address these demands (Senge, et al., 2010). Seeing the larger picture requires looking at the value created. Also, LCA modeling identifies waste as a resource and the how efficiency in one area can lead to inefficiencies for other areas.

Sustainable Value Framework Analysis

Sustainability embraces living today without damaging tomorrow (Senage, Smith, Kruschwitz, Laur, & Schley, 2008). The quest for sustainability involves risks and opportunities. Doing nothing and maintaining the status quo is no longer a viable option in business. According to Senge (2008), aligning priorities with new realities are vital (Senge, 2008 p. 103). More and more people in the business world accept the global changes and changes here in the United States surrounding sustainability. For sustainability to happen leaders with solutions must implement these solutions effectively.

Strategic thinking supports innovation. However, for true innovation to occur thinking differently is required (Senge, 2008). Leaders at Starbucks must have a strategy that includes degrees of detail, interaction, dynamic phenomena, and paradoxical phenomena (Stacey, 2011). Each topic noted is concerned with ways of thinking about how firms change over time. What is known about good business is that it changes with the times to stay relevant (Press, 2005).

When businesses are searching for sustainable solutions, a key strategy is to collaborate with unconventional allies (Senge, 2008). Starbucks CEO Howard Schultz collaborated with Oprah Winfrey to launch the "Teavana Oprah Chai Tea" this year (Starbucks, 2014). Here we have an unlikely venture, two journeys, and one destination. The destination for both parties is confronting a basic need (Senge, 2008). The CEO of Starbucks seeks to increase market-share while Oprah Winfrey seeks to stay current and in the public eye.

Detailed Analysis of All Four Quadrants

Table 2: Sustainable Value Framework

	Today	Future
External	Strategy: Product Stewardship-Starbucks Sustainable Packaging Designs and Materials, Sustainably Sourced Products Payoff: Increases brand recognition and reputation among coffee retailers, and establishes legitimacy with shareholders.	Strategy: Sustainability vision-Starbucks Code of Ethics, Vendor Code of Conduct, Community Relations, and Commitment Mission, Greenhouse Gas Reduction program. Payoff: Sustainable operations for long-term viability and growth
Internal	Strategy: Pollution prevention- Starbucks Energy program for efficiency, Conservation and recycling programs Payoff: Lower risks and costs associated with warehouse facilities	Strategy: Clean technology-Starbucks Mission and LEED Certification Payoff: Innovative buildings that strengthen positioning for future viability.

Conclusion

The Starbucks Corporation vision captures and aligns their strategic planning to meet performance goals. The firm has warehouse efficiencies and operational effectiveness. Moreover, strives for sustainable future, elects programs, and measures to further progress. Also, expanding overseas to drive future profitability may limit their specific interests in nations or countries with larger or growing GDP.

Also, to setting stringent code of ethics when establishing partnerships and some countries do not have the same laws protecting Starbucks vision. The firm consistently sales high-quality products and has a matchless return policy, with a reputation and brand to match. The expansion is one of many strategies available to Starbucks while determined to focus on keeping satisfied consumers. The firms' future profitability and overall strength rely on the leadership's team ability to lead ongoing unpredictable changes occurring in the economic, global, and political environments.

References

Albors-Garrigos, J. d. (2014). Positioning in the Global Value Chain as a Sustainable Strategy: A Case Study in a Mature Industry. *Administrative Sciences*, 2076-3387), 4(2), 155-172. doi:10.3390/admsci4020155.

Brain, S. (2014, July 12). *Starbucks Company Statistics*. Retrieved from http://www.statisticbrain.com/starbucks-company-statistics/

Dunkin' Donuts. (2011, 12 19). Retrieved from Dunkin' Donuts: http://www.dunkindonuts.com/content/dunkindonuts/en/company.html

Forbes. (2013, December 19). *Forbes.com*. Retrieved from http://www.forbes.com

IBIS, W. (2014, 9 1). *The Coffee and Snack Shop Industry in the US Report*. Retrieved from https://www.ibisworld.com

Janićijević, N. (2013). The mutual impact of organizational culture and structure. *Ekonomski Anali / Economic Annals*, 35-60. doi: 10.2298/EKA1398035J.

Markides, C. (2012). Think again fine turning your strategic thinking. *Business Strategy Review*, 23(4), 80-85. doi:10.1111/j.1467-8616.2012.00910.x.

Merriam-Webster. (2014, 9 6). Retrieved from http://www.merriam-webster.com/dictionary/symbiosis

Marriott, B. (2007, September 12). *Starbucks coffee and Marriott hotels*. Retrieved from http://www.blogs.marriott.com

McDonald's Corporation. (2014, 9 2). Retrieved from McDonald's Corporation: http://www.mcdonalds.com

Miller, C. C. (2009, January 29). *The New York Times*. Retrieved from The New York Times: http://www.nytimes.com

Mintzberg, H. &. (1999). Reflecting on the strategy process. *Sloan Management Review*, 40 (3), 21-30.

NetMBA. (2010). The value chain. Retrieved from http://www.netmba.com/strategy/value-chain

Porter, M. E. (1985). How Information gives you a competitive advantage. *Harvard Business Review*, 63 (4), 149-160.

Press, H. B. (2005). *Strategy: Create and implement the best strategy for your business.* Boston, MA: Author.

Senge, P. S. (2008). *The necessary revolution: Working together to create a sustainable world.* New York, NY: Broadway Books.

Senge, P., Smith, B., Kruschwitz, N., Laur, J., & Schley, S. (2010*). The necessary revolution: How individuals and organizations are working together to create a sustainable world.* Double day, NY: Random House, Inc.

Stacey, R., (2011). *Strategic management and organisational dynamics: The challenge of complexity.* (6th ed.) Harlow, England: Pearson Education Limited.

Stainback, S. a. (1988). *Conducting a Qualitative Research Study. Understanding and conducting qualitative research.* Reston, VA: Council for Exceptional Children.

Starbucks, I. (2014, August 2). *Starbucks.com.* Retrieved from http://www.starbucks.com/about-us/company-information

Starbucks, I. (2014, September 22). *Starbucks.com.* Retrieved from http://www.starbucks.com/facts-Healthcare

Times, S. (2014, 9 02). *Seattle Times.* Retrieved from http://seattletimes.com

University, G. M. (2014, 8 19). *College of Education and Human Development*.

Retrieved from http://gse.gmu.edu/research/tr/tr-process/tr-conclusions

Yaqalla, M. (2014, May 2). *Starbucks Continues to Blow Away the Competition*.

Retrieved from http://www.fool.com

Additional Material and Contact Information

Dr. Enid A. Thompson has also authored the following books:

- I'm Coming For You

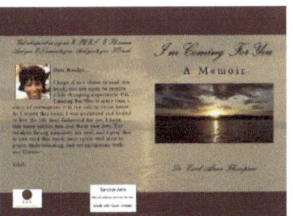

- Managing Effective Communication After a Crisis

- Organizational Change and Employee Retention: Strange Bedfellows

- Quantitative Decision-Making for Business Analysis

Her new book entitled "Let's Get Busy" will be released early 2018. "Let's Get Busy" is

the sequel in the New Earth Series from Dr. Enid as a follow-up to "What Now?" This book is an in-depth look how each of us has a role in creating the new systems we all desire in the educational and legislative branch of our country. Interested in booking Dr. Thompson as a speaker, email her team at dr.enid@yahoo.com or by calling Guide Consultants (813) 563-2076. Dr. Enid lives in Wesley Chapel, Florida with her husband, James. They have two adult children and two grandchildren. For more information about Dr. Enid and her work go to www.consultwithdrenid.com

The New Earth Series Presents

Sustainable Solutions for a Successful Business

By

Dr. Enid Alane Thompson

Published by CreateSpace Self-Publishing (LLC), an Amazon Company, and Kindle

Direct Publishing (LLC) Copyright of Book is held by the Author.

2016